FAVORITE HORSES

Coloring Book

JOHN GREEN

DOVER PUBLICATIONS, INC.
Mineola, New York

NOTE

For thousands of years horses have played an important part in human history. Strong and swift, they have pulled plows, hauled heavy loads, and carried soldiers into battle. Hitched to carts and carriages, they have provided transportation for people over the centuries. As racing horses and rodeo performers, these appealing animals have entertained countless thousands. This book invites you to color thirty different kinds of horses–from the beloved Shetland Pony to the swift and graceful Thoroughbred. Identifying captions give brief descriptions of each breed and its characteristics.

LIST OF HORSES

Copyright

Copyright © 2005 by Dover Publications, Inc.
All rights reserved.

Bibliographical Note

Favorite Horses Coloring Book is a new work, first published by Dover Publications, Inc., in 2005.

DOVER *Pictorial Archive* SERIES

International Standard Book Number: 0-486-44010-9

Manufactured in the United States of America
Dover Publications, Inc., 31 East 2nd Street, Mineola, N.Y. 11501

The **Andalusian** horse comes from the province of Andalusia in southern Spain. It has been known since ancient times as one of the best horses for use in battle.

Recognized by their spotted coats, **Appaloosas** were highly prized
by the Nez Perce Indians of the American Northwest.

The beautiful **Arabian** horse originated long ago in the deserts of the
Middle East, bred by tribes of wandering peoples called Bedouins.

The **Canadian** horse was first brought to Canada from France in the seventeenth century. Today, its strength and endurance make it a favorite with the Royal Canadian Mounted Police.

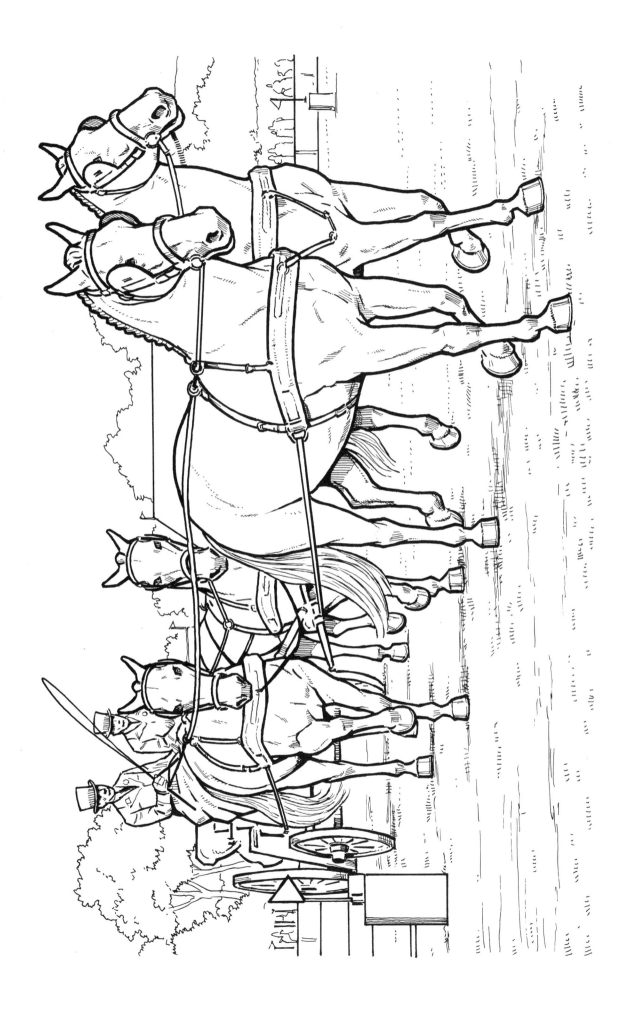

One of the oldest breeds of English horses, the **Cleveland Bay** is distinguished by its reddish-brown color, as well as its black mane, tail, and legs.

The **Clydesdale** is a large Scottish horse developed for hauling heavy loads.
A full-grown stallion can weigh up to 2,200 pounds.

The typical horse used by the New York City Mounted Police is a **Crossbreed**—a chestnut or bay gelding that can tolerate the noise and crowding of the city.

Crossbreed working horses play an important role in British royal ceremonies. They are mainly Cleveland Bays or **Windsor Greys.** The Greys are not a specific breed, but horses selected for appearance and temperament.

Known for its strength and spirit, the **Danish Warmblood** excels in such competitions as dressage (a series of carefully performed movements testing the horse's training and the rider's control) and cross-country events.

One of the oldest Russian riding horses, the **Don** breed was
developed by the Cossack peoples of southern Russia.

A large, even-tempered animal, the British **Drum Horse** carries a rider
and two solid silver kettle drums during parades and events.

The **Friesian** horse originated centuries ago in the Netherlands when medieval knights used to ride them into battle. Today, these beautiful black horses are used to pull coaches and carriages on special occasions.

One of the best-known riding breeds in the world, the German **Hanoverian** is
noble and well-proportioned, with natural balance and a calm disposition.

Known as far back as Viking times, the Danish **Knabstrup** (above) sports a beautiful, spotted coat. It is a calm and friendly horse, often found in circuses. One of the oldest horse breeds in Britain, the **Shetland Pony** (below) originated in the Shetland Islands off the coast of Scotland. Strong and gentle, it is among the most popular ponies in the world.

Exceptionally kind, intelligent, and willing to learn, Austrian **Lipizzaners** are famous for their dressage routines (precise, dancelike movements guided by slight signals from the rider) performed at the Spanish Riding School in Vienna.

Related to the Andalusian horse of Spain, the Portuguese **Lusitano**
is used in bullfighting and as a general riding horse.

The **Missouri Fox Trotter** was developed in the rugged Ozark Mountains during the nineteenth century by settlers who needed sure-footed, easy-riding horses that could travel long distances.

The **Morgan** horse began in eighteenth-century Massachusetts with a horse given to Justin Morgan, a Vermont school-teacher. This American breed became widely known and admired for its strength, versatility, and all-around usefulness.

Still roaming the American West today, **Mustangs** are wild horses descended from horses brought by Spanish explorers in the 1500s.

19

Russia's most famous breed of horse, the **Orlov Trotter** began in the eighteenth century as a harness-racing horse known for speed and endurance.

Palomino horses boast a golden coat with white mane and tail and are popular in parades, rodeos, movies, and on television. "Palomino" is not actually a breed, but a color, and such horses as Morgans, American Saddlebreds, and Arabians can all be "palominos."

Bred for size, weight, and strength, the **Percheron** of France was a
favorite for hauling heavy loads around the farm.

Introduced to North America by European explorers, the swift and lively
Pinto was a popular mount with Native Americans.

The first breed native to the United States, the **Quarter Horse** was named for
its ability to run very fast in a quarter-mile race. Its calm disposition and
"cow sense" helped make it an excellent ranch horse as well.

American Saddlebreds are descended from British horses shipped to North America in the 1600s. Used for riding, plowing, pulling carriages, and other work, they combine an easy riding gait, strength, and stamina.

The **Selle Français,** or French Saddle Horse, is one of the finest sport horses in the world. This breed does very well in international show jumping.

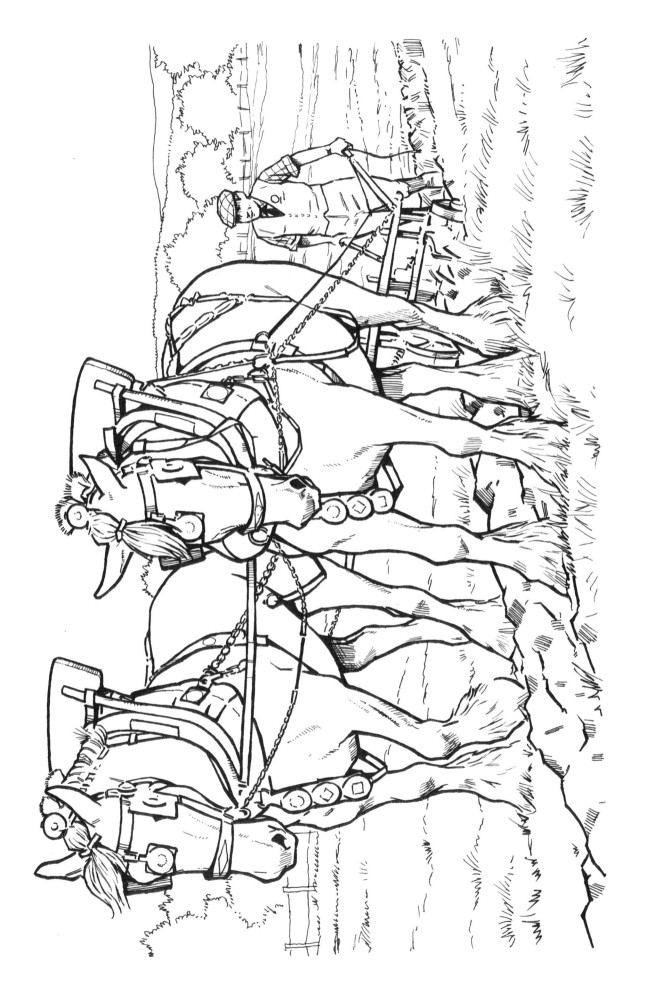

Descended from the medieval "Great Horse," the large and powerful English **Shire** horse is ideal for hauling heavy loads or pulling a plow.

Dating back just over 200 years, **Standardbreds** were so named because early trotters were required to reach a certain "standard" for the mile distance. Today, the Standardbred is the fastest harness-racing horse in the world.

Developed in eastern England to handle heavy farmwork, the **Suffolk Punch** breed of draft horse boasts great strength, endurance, and an easygoing temperament.

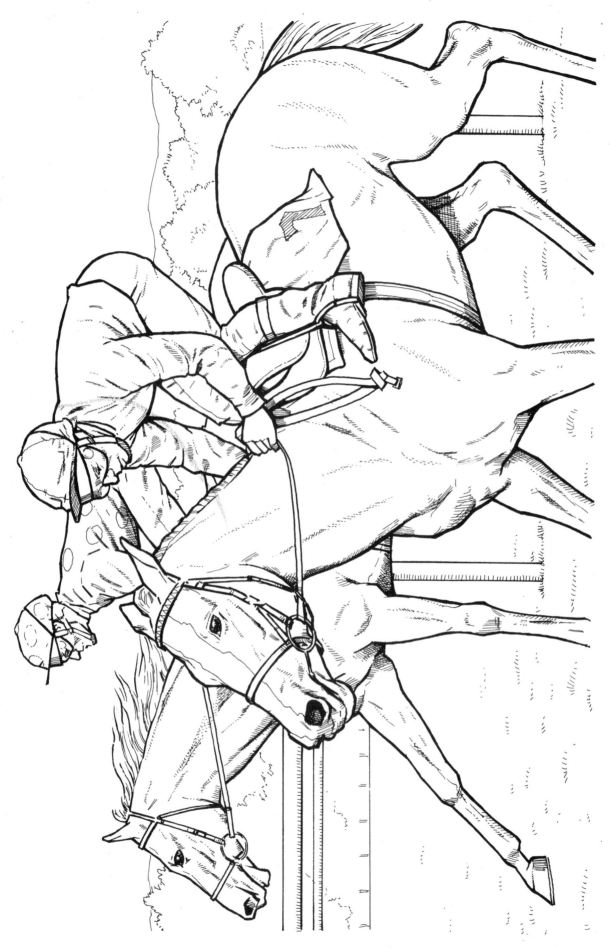

Properly known as the English Running Horse, the **Thoroughbred** is the fastest of all horses, capable of running for a mile at almost 40 miles per hour.